Up Shit Creek

Up Shit Creek

A Collection of Horrifyingly True Wilderness Toilet Misadventures

Joe Lindsay

Ten Speed Press
BERKELEY, CALIFORNIA

Ten Speed Press
P.O. Box 7123
Berkeley, California 94707
www.tenspeed.com

Distributed in Australia by Simon and Schuster Australia, in Canada by Ten Speed Press Canada, in New Zealand by Southern Publishers Group, in South Africa by Real Books, and in the United Kingdom and Europe by Airlift Book Company.

Interior design and typesetting by Jeff Brandenburg/ImageComp
Cover design by Cale Burr
Illustrations by Gary O'Brien
Cover photographs by Jonathan Chester (background) and
    Mike Lane (inset)
Cover model: Mark Krebs

Library of Congress Cataloging-in-Publication Data
Lindsay, Joe.
        Up shit creek: a collection of horrifyingly true wilderness
    toilet misadventures / Joe Lindsay
                p.   cm.
        ISBN-10: 0-89815-939-3 (pbk.)
        ISBN-13: 978-0-89815-939-4 (pbk.)
        1. Rafting (Sports)—Humor. 2. Toilets—Humor. 3. Feces—
Humor. I. Title.
GV780.L56 1997
797.1'21'0207—dc21   97-9464
                                        CIP

Printed in the United States of America

11 12 13 14 15 — 09 08 07 06 05

For Karl Mueggler and Max Lyon—*my evil brothers*

Visit the author at her website:
www.KathleenintheWoods.com

Contents

Acknowledgments

This book really started as a joke—something to occupy and entertain me last spring when I dropped out of college for a while. I am most thankful and amazed that it is now a real book and I am sitting here writing these acknowledgments just like a real writer. The stories are not mine but belong to the river and to all of the impish, child-like river guides who make the canyons and waters their home. Now, I need to acknowledge a few people here in this acknowledgments section since that is what we real writers do.

To Mom, "Macha del rio," for guiding me down my first river when I was eight years old and introducing me to its wonders. To Bill Lindsay, my amazing, smart father for the stories he would spin out of thin mountain air. To Spence, my big brother with a big brain. I marvel at you. To magnificent Deborah, Kaya, and Kenna—my sister and nieces. I love you all.

To Looper, Ursula, Tim Adams, Jim Ritter, Jeff Kellog, the Knade, Animal Kokinos, Heidi Ho, Bishy, Bri Bri, Bozmo, Glenn, Andy Anderson, Mi Mi, Kimba who I had a huge crush on, Bill and Deanna, Uncle Phil Finkel and the mooon; the residents of campsite E, Julie, Mark, and Kelly—the Futuleafu source-to-sea team. To the guides of the Kern Valley, the Tuolumne, the Middle Fork Salmon, and all other streams.

To Kathy Meyer for encouraging me to explore the world of the wilderness poop story.

To Clancy Drake, my editor, and to Ten Speed Press for having faith in this goofy book.

To Robert Stricker, my hep agent.

To Dr. Carl Fullbright for helping me with some crappy research.

To Jim Dodge for reading the original manuscript and spending his valuable time talking shit with me. To Gary O'Brien for his amazing illustrations, creativity, friendship, and collaboration on our brief rap music career.

To Rusty Grim for encouraging me to write the first of these stories and for being my friend during a particularly chilly, dark winter. To Theo, Jane, and Taku for the talks, the sandwiches at Guernika, and the runs in the hills. To Russ Stoddard for first publishing "The Birth of the Groover."

To my friends. To Hainers, Kerrin, and Do-die. To those of us who loved Karl and Max. To Evil Brother Peter and Evil Sister Evans. To Mike Cohen and the Red Lion of Judah. To Erin and Sin Sin; mi amigo Andrés! To brother Bill for his thoughts and ruminations over oatmeal eaten on the porch. To Mitz-eye, Zan and Marcie, Heather, Jeffrey, Krista, and Indy. To Eileen, John Farmer and Tracey, Mighty Mike Good, Cheryl, Mike and Heather, Tom, Jan and Dave Lyon, and the crew at L.D.'s that morning. That was magic.

Introduction

Working as a commercial river guide for the last ten years, I have grown to appreciate the colorful oral tradition of the river-running community. There are many stories surrounding rivers, and there is nothing more enjoyable after a day of floating through pristine wilderness than sitting around a crackling fire, looking into the glowing face of a skilled storyteller, and listening to a well-spun yarn complete with hand gestures and lots of exaggeration and fabrication.

There are many kinds of tales in the river guide's repertoire: gnarly rapid lore, wild animal encounter stories, human history stories, Native American legends, and so on. There are also the more significant river legends—mythic, archetypal stories of quest and growth like *Siddhartha* and *Huckleberry Finn*. Then there are stories of a decidedly less literary nature. I am referring, of course, to river toilet or **"groover"** tales. Of these there are many, ranging from the cute and innocent to the blatantly vile and disgusting. While *Up Shit Creek* offers a varied selection along this continuum, I must admit that the majority of these stories lean toward the vile and disgusting.

In order to help you make wise decisions for yourself and your stomach, I have devised a very scientific rating system, modeled after the classification system for whitewater rapids: from class I—flat moving water—to class VI—unrunnable, teeth-gnashing, bone-crunching cataracts and waterfalls. Instead of "class," I have decided to use "rolls" (of toilet paper) to indicate the severity of the groover tale. It breaks down like this:

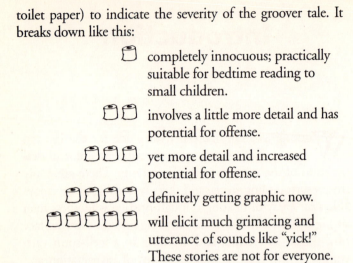

completely innocuous; practically suitable for bedtime reading to small children.

involves a little more detail and has potential for offense.

yet more detail and increased potential for offense.

definitely getting graphic now.

will elicit much grimacing and utterance of sounds like "yick!" These stories are not for everyone.

actual nausea is the most common reaction.

Now, if you are to appreciate these stories to their fullest, you must have some basic information in addition to this rating system. For example, you need to know what a groover is.

Simply put, a groover is a container of some kind into which river runners deposit their number twos. Groovers come in a variety of shapes and sizes and have different accessory packages, but their basic function remains the same: they are turd tanks. The different models of groovers mentioned in this book are diagrammed and intricately labeled in chapter one, "Styles of Groovers." I encourage you to examine these diagrams, as they will most likely enhance your understanding and enjoyment of the tales.

Some people, upon hearing that they must poop in a box, question whether it is really necessary to take such precautions. In the early 1900s, when there were only a few loners, miners, and fur traders inhabiting our river canyons, groovers were not necessary. But today, with the increased popularity of wilderness outfitting, there are literally thousands of people floating and packing through certain sections of river canyon and wilderness each year. If each of them left a few loaves in every camp it would not be long before serious problems developed. The canyons that we float through would look and smell quite different were it not for the groover.

Here's an example. The Grand Canyon of the Colorado River is rafted by approximately 23,000 people every river season. The average person leaves about a half-pound of doo-doo behind each day, depending on how much fiber is in his or her diet. In one season, in the less than one hundred camps in Grand Canyon, there would be 115,000 *pounds* of shit left behind if it were not packed out. That's about 1,000 pounds per camp. Things don't decompose too quickly in such an arid environment. Those turds would pile up fast and would remain for some time.

There are other, more lofty benefits to the groover. In this age of hectic schedules and power lunches, the groover offers us a certain connectedness to our bodies, the wilderness, and our place in it. When we sit on the seat out in the wilds, amongst the grasses and bushes of river canyons, we slow down. We notice the birds soaring above us in the early morning light; we have time to relax and appreciate where we are. In fact, at the end of many river trips, guests have told me that they will miss the groover and the peace they found thereon.

Of course, these are usually people who have not experienced the darker side of the groover. That is where the tales in this book come into the picture. These stories are funny, but they are also pretty twisted. If you use the rating system to tailor your selections, you will have many laughs. But be forewarned that your laughter may be mixed with grimaces and utterances of such words as "gads," "gross," and "eeew."

Also, I must make a disclaimer at this point. Please know that the groover is a tool that river-runners use to reduce their impact on the wilderness. Ninety-nine percent of the time these systems work beautifully and nary a drop nor dollop of human waste is spilt. But, as in any system, there are sometimes frightful mishaps and malfunctions: these are the exception and not the rule. Some of these stories include scenes that are less than friendly to the environment, and some of the characters might seem to be environmentally callous—or, worse yet, malicious. Please know that river outfitters and guides are very respectful and sensitive to their environment and would never take pleasure in any fecal polluting of the waterways they love.

Note: Throughout this book, you will find a number of words that may be unfamiliar—rafting terms and so forth. Many of these are collected in the glossary on page 79; the first time they appear in each chapter, they are **bold**.

April 14, 1997
Arcata, California

1

Styles of Groovers

The stories in this book deal with four different kinds of **groover**: the classic with bags, the classic without bags, the Jon-ny Partner, and the Millennium Falcon. For your further education and reading enjoyment, these groovers are described and illustrated below.

The Classic with Bags

Here you see the classic groover with bags. This system lives up to its name: it has been the most commonly used

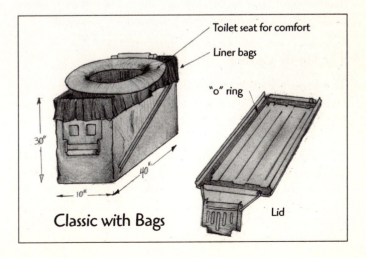

Toilet seat for comfort

Liner bags

"o" ring

30"

40"

10"

Classic with Bags

Lid

groover for quite some time now. The classic is a metal **rocket box** which can be purchased at military surplus stores for around twenty dollars. It has a clamp-down lid with an O-ring to keep it watertight. A toilet seat is usually placed over the can when the groover is set up, making for a more comfortable poop-session.

Large, thirty-three-gallon garbage bags are used with this system to control the smell and keep things contained; the box is lined with *at least* two of them when it is set up. When the classic groover is broken down in the morning by a lucky river guide, the bags are first **burped** of their air (said guide's head is usually turned to the side for this), and then sealed with knots. The resulting object is called a **pod**, a nice, neat little package of human waste sealed in plastic—the fruit of the classic. As the classic has long been one of the most commonly used systems, the box and the resulting pods are at the center of many of these tales.

The Classic Without Bags

This version of the classic is a little less sweet-smelling and neatly organized. With this groover, number twos are deposited directly into the can and remain there for all to see, as there are no folds of brown plastic for the turds to hide behind. It is a no-frills, in-your-face style of groover that makes no attempt to be anything other than what it is—a can of poop. There are no pods produced by this system.

The Jon-ny Partner

The Jon-ny Partner is a truly fine groover system and is widely considered to be one of the more upscale wilderness toilets available. The rafting company I work for* just recently adopted it as its standard groover, and most of my experiences with the Jon-ny Partner have been quite good.

The system consists of a square steel tank and a toilet seat insert that fits into the tank. When the insert is

---

* Outdoor Adventures, whose guides and groovers will be featured in several of these tales, including "Swirlies at His Ankles" and "The Groover That Ate Sonora."

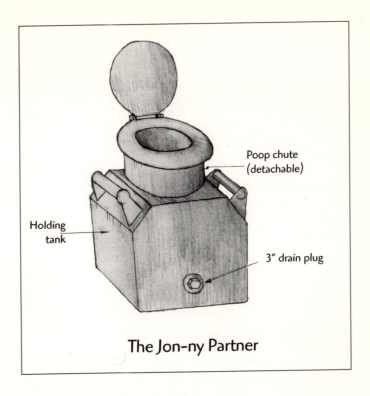

Poop chute (detachable)

Holding tank

3" drain plug

The Jon-ny Partner

removed, a lid with an O-ring clamps down over the hole, sealing in shit and accompanying smells. At the tank's base there is a small, three-inch hole sealed with a black rubber plug; this is for blasting water into the tank to flush out the inside after its contents are removed.

The Millennium Falcon

The Millennium Falcon is named for its resemblance to the famous spaceship piloted by Han Solo in the *Star Wars* films. It is a strangely shaped plastic box—six inches high and about two and a half feet square. The toilet seat assembly is a permanent fixture on the Falcon and cannot be removed. The pedal on the side of the holding tank operates as a flushing mechanism, opening a trap door into the holding tank for turds to fall through.

The Millennium Falcon

Flushing pedal

2

The Birth of the Groover

Groover Type: *Classic*
Rating: 🧻

Legend has it that the nickname for the river porta-potty, "groover," was coined on a river trip down the Colorado River through Grand Canyon in the late 1970s. The specific trip date and the names of its participants are not known but the events that transpired on those eighteen blistering days shaped a river tradition that will undoubtedly live on past those mortals whose flaws contributed to its birth.

The most common **"pooper"** system in those days—and indeed one which even now enjoys much popularity—was the tried-and-true rocket box system. It consists of a military rocket box in which to store the **goodness**, an odor retardant such as crystallized bleach or **blue goo**, and a toilet seat. The rafters in question were using such a system.

It seems that the person on this mythic trip who was entrusted with the responsibility of assembling this system forgot the toilet seat—a most integral part of the system. This situation was of course discovered on the first evening, when the unwary adventurers, camped in Marble Canyon, were relaxing and rubbing their stomachs after some particularly tasty enchiladas. They soon realized they had to venture into (or onto) uncharted territory—a pooper without seat. So that bravest and most desperate first rafter ventured to the secluded, sandy spot behind the **tamarisk**, sat down upon the throne sans seat, and "did his business."

Upon returning to the rest of the group, cut-off shorts hoisted into place, this recently relieved member of the party was noticed to have deep grooves running down the backs of his thighs, marking where he had been sitting upon the seatless rocket box. This then became the telltale mark of a visit to the toilet—those grooves in the thighs. Hence the name: **viva la Groover!**

3

Turd Sandwich

Groover Type: *Classic with Bags*
Rating: 🧻 🧻 🧻

What follows is a story that has been passed down
from guide to guide at Outdoor Adventures for
several years—achieving almost mythic status. I feel
that it is one of the most compelling, disgusting, and
truly amazing tales in these pages—but you, of
course, will have to judge this for yourself. While it is
somewhat horrifying, many have found it
entertaining and worthy of many retellings. Keep in
mind, though, that "Turd Sandwich" is not for
everyone: this tale has been awarded three rolls of
T.P. Those who are not prepared for "Turd
Sandwich" should read no further, but the fecally
fascinated, must, of course, read on. It is your duty.

It was a fine spring day on the forks of the Kern, a rather
impressive stretch of Class IV and V whitewater in the
southern Sierra Nevada. The sun was shining and there was
a crispness to the air. Keith Knadler, a guide for Outdoor
Adventures, sat looking through his amber shades at the
river as it slid powerfully by. The leaves of the aspen trees

that surrounded him in a small amphitheater were flickering in the cool wind of the morning and the steady rumble of the river soothed him. The toilet seat had been cold when he first sat down but had warmed up now. He was comfortable—enjoying the grandeur of glaciated Kern Canyon and feeling the sun on his face. It was indeed a fine morning.

The Forks of the Kern is a special section of river as it has no road to its **put-in**. All the gear and food, with the exception of the rafters' personal gear, is packed down a two-mile trail into Kern Canyon on the backs of mules. The logistics of running a commercial trip on the Forks are kind of interesting for this reason. The lead guide does not come down the trail with the rest of the guides and the gear the night before the trip, but stays in Kernville that day, meets the guests, and gives them a safety talk and a swim test to determine if they are in adequate shape to raft the Forks.

The following morning, the lead guide loads all of the folks on the bus for the two-hour drive on winding roads up past the town of Johnsondale and into the high, crisp altitudes of the Golden Trout Wilderness. At the end of the bus ride, they reach the trailhead amongst the incense cedars and ponderosa pines, load their waterproof bags on their backs, and head down the trail to the put-in. There they are greeted by the other guides, who have been busy slicing, dicing, and artfully arranging vegetables and deli items for the first lunch.

Keith sat a little longer thinking of the rapids that lay ahead, then wiped, rose, and hoisted his nylon river shorts. He breathed deeply, dipped a ladle of hand wash water, hooked it to the side of the **bail bucket**, and felt the chill of the icy water flow over his sudsy hands. Shaking them off and wiping them on his shorts, he put his hands to his mouth and cried out the requisite morning warning, "Last call on the groover!"

"I'm done, Keith," replied Heidi as she cleaned up the morning oatmeal pot and munched on a bagel with cream cheese. Heidi and Keith had come down to the river the night before and were now preparing for their day of rigging the rafts, assembling the **oar frames**, and organizing the food for the trip. Jeff Pfleuger, the lead guide, and Tom, a young and enthusiastic guide-in-training, would be coming in that afternoon with the guests.

"OK, Heidi. I'll tie it up," said Keith.

And he did. But just *how* he tied it up is at the root of this tale. You must understand that, when breaking down the classic groover, one must tie rather tight knots in the bags for two reasons: one, it would be disgusting and dangerous to have any leakage of the **goodness**; and, two, these tight knots serve to communicate the contents of the bag. A tightly tied knot in a bulging garbage bag pulled from a reeking rocket box can contain only one thing. This bag with the tight knot says, "Don't untie me. I am filled with pestilence." But that morning, Keith decided for some reason not to follow protocol as he broke down the groover. He tied knots in the bags, but these were not tight knots. They were loose ones—very loose. If he had known then what was to happen just a few hours later, no doubt he would have made another decision. He finished the breakdown and returned to the beach to continue rigging the rafts. The loosely tied knots rested—no, waited—in the groover.

Some hours later, Jeff and Tom came down the trail with the guests. Heidi and Keith were preparing lunch, the boats were rigged, and the sun was out. It was a fine day and everyone was looking forward to the class V whitewater that was to come. Jeff finished his paddle talk and made last preparations for the afternoon on the river. . . meanwhile, the knots waited.

The rapids that day were as thrilling and stomach butterfly-inducing as ever. There were no mishaps, as this was the crew's fifth trip down the river that season and all felt comfortable. Even Tom, training in the **gear raft**, had fine runs and a great time. They pulled into the Needlerock camp **eddy** around three o'clock—perfect timing.

In my many years of river running, I have never seen a camp quite as beautiful as Needlerock. It seems to have it all: a beach, multiple flat tent spots, a class V rapid above and below with a calm pool between, a view of the Needles—granite spires that shoot several thousand feet above the canyon, and the final touch, Needle Rock Falls, a tumbling streak of white down a granite dome into the river right across from the beach. It is truly an amazing camp.

Back to our story. Once at the camp, Jeff, Heidi, Keith, and Tom untied the gear that they had lashed to their rafts and started a "fire line," passing bags, tents, stoves, and propane bottles up to the kitchen area in bucket brigade fashion. Tom untied the groover and set it on the beach beside his raft.

The knots waited.

"Hey Tom, have you ever set up the groover?"

"No, I haven't, Jeff."

"Well, let's go. I'll show you how it's done."

"Great!"

So off they went to another of Needlerock's many treasures—the most idyllic groover spot on the planet, with an uncompromised view of Needlerock rapid, the Needles, and, of course, the waterfall. This is an especially inspiring spot in the morning, with the **alpenglow** warming up the canyon, some coffee in one's hand, and the sound of Good Morning Rapid thrashing in the canyon below. Jeff forged on up the trail and Tom followed with the groover.

"First thing you do is pop off the lid. But remember to hold your nose," said Jeff with a chuckle as he pulled on the latches holding the metal lid in place. "Now you take out the **blue goo**, the toilet seat and the . . ."—grabbing the bag with the loose knots—". . . toilet paper. See, Tom, we put stuff we don't want getting wet in garbage bags," he said, holding the loose knots in his left hand. "This is the toilet paper in here."

"All right. Got it. Toilet paper in garbage bags."

Jeff continued *untying* the knots and opening the bags—"I'll just get the toilet paper out of here . . ."—reaching *into the bags*—". . . Aw, man—they didn't tie these knots tight enough. The toilet paper got all wet."

At that moment, Jeff was unknowingly living the nightmare of many commercial river guides: actually touching—indeed, firmly grasping—the treats left by another.

He pulled what he thought was wet toilet paper from the bags, "I guess we'll just have to let it dr. . . ."

A silence fell then. The river roared behind the two guides and a breeze blew through the cedar branches above their heads.

Jeff stood frozen in silent horror, eyes locked on what was gripped between the fingers of his right hand: a cylinder of human poop wrapped neatly in moist toilet paper—a turd sandwich. He remained mute, gripped with fear and shock, looking down the business end of that caca sandwich.

It was Tom who snapped out of it first, moving quickly to save his friend and trainer. His words were meaningful, inspiring, and to the point:

"PUT THAT BACK!!!"

The spell broken, Jeff began to scream, "AHHHHH-HHH!!," stuffing his hand back in the bag, returning the shit sandwich to whence it came. He then ran, frantically stumbling in a straight line over boulders and through willows, arms and legs flailing for balance as he crashed down the bank to the river, throwing himself with a wail into the cleansing waters of the Kern. It is said that he stayed there for twenty minutes, frantically scrubbing and yelling many foul and unmentionable things.

To this day on Outdoor Adventures trips on the Forks of the Kern, the bags of turds are tied with tight, decisive knots, and my pal Jeff does not often put his hand into mysterious garbage bags.

4

The Sting

Groover Type: *Classic with Bags*
Rating: 🧻 🧻 🧻

This tale was told to me by Frank, a veteran
Salmon River guide who I met one day while
browsing through the shorts and T-shirt rack at an
outdoor store in Salmon, Idaho. He had a look that
spoke of many years on the river and I imagined
he was a rather deft spinner of yarn. I asked him
for a tale and he gave me the three-roll gem that
follows. Frank had heard this story through the
guidevine and so had only sketchy details for me: I
have filled in some information here and there, but
the basic facts remain the same.*

It was a small trip on the Main Salmon River—only eight
guests and two guides. It was night four of the trip and
things had been going fairly well, but both guides felt that
there was something missing.

---

*While this story does detail what seems to be a rather cruel joke played on
some unsuspecting commercial guests, Frank assured me that it was taken
well and there were no hard feelings afterwards.

"These people are duds."

"They're nice, but I know what you mean—sort of lifeless, huh?"

"Yeah."

They stood next to each other looking at the circle of guests sitting in their camp chairs on the beach. Their eyes watered from the onions they were chopping and the long prep table where they worked was dotted with plates piled high with sliced mushrooms, grated mozzarella, olives, and sautéed Italian sausage. The night's fare would be lasagna, bread, and Caesar salad—a favorite meal on most trips. The guides had doubts that these folks would even notice the meal. It was just one of those trips that lacked chemistry—maybe the guests were having fun, but it was tough for the guides to tell—even on the fourth night.

Brownies would be served for dessert.

The guests sat in their small and silent circle, reading books and magazines, eyes buried in print. The afternoon light was slanting into the canyon and the river slid slowly by. An osprey flapped its wings for balance in the crown of a ponderosa pine just across the river, then glided off its perch, hovering fifty feet above the river, its white wings beating until it spotted its quarry, a rainbow trout, in the waters below. Both guides watched in silence as the bird folded its wings and plummeted like a smooth, speckled stone into the green water with a splash, emerging moments later with the prize dangling from its talons.

One of the guests heard the splash, looked up from his *New Yorker* momentarily, then returned to his reading with a shrug.

"We have to do something. This is getting ridiculous."

"Maybe we could shock them out of it somehow."

"Are we having brownies for dessert?"

"Yeah."

"I have a plan."

Dinner was served around 7:30 that evening to a polite but unenthusiastic reception. The lasagna was tasty, as were the bread and Caesar salad; soon everyone was so stuffed with dinner that very few had room for dessert. The guides had cooked up a double batch of brownies and the **Dutch oven** was loaded with gooey, moist chocolate treats. Only one or two of the guests took small pieces so there were plenty of leftovers. As the guests brushed their teeth and prepared for bed, the guides carefully placed the under-cooked brownies, with their pudding-like centers, in a Ziploc bag and tucked them into a cooler. Nervous laughter rippled from two shadowed figures in the camp kitchen. The plan was underway.

The next morning came clear and crisp; it was nearing the end of August and it was evident that fall was quickly approaching. The coffee was particularly strong that morning and did a fine job of waking up the bleary-eyed guides and guests. It also seemed to be a busier-than-normal morning at the groover.

It was obvious to the guests that there was a certain tension between the two guides that morning and that they seemed to be snapping at each other more often than not. Otherwise, they worked silently and efficiently, breaking down the kitchen, the shade tarp, and the chairs as the guests prepared for another day on the river, slathering themselves with sunscreen and sitting quietly on the beach. They didn't notice when one of the guides grabbed the bag of brownies from the cooler and hid the package beneath his T-shirt, shoving it into the belt strap of his shorts. He walked up the beach past the guests and toward the other guide, who was carrying a food box down to the boats.

"Hey, I think everyone's done with the groover. Go break it down," ordered the guide with the box of food.

"Why don't *you* do it? I've broken it down every morning this trip," said Brownie Guide.

"Too bad. Quit sniveling and go break it down—I'm busy," said the other, abruptly turning and walking down the beach.

The guests had all seen and heard the conversation and it made them uncomfortable to see their guides interacting in such a manner. They watched quietly as the noticeably disturbed food box guide quickly tied his load to his raft, mumbling something about being tired of "working with nimrods."

Meanwhile, up the groover trail, Brownie Guide had almost finished the break-down; he was working with a classic groover with bags. He had **burped the bags**, and tied the knots, and now he was flattening the **pods**, getting them to settle evenly in the can. Since this was the morning of the fifth day of a six-day trip, the box was about seven-eighths full of turd pods, leaving just about an inch of air-space. After flattening and settling the bags, he reached under his shirt and removed the bag of brownies. He opened it and spread the sticky substrate evenly over the plastic poo pods within the groover, effectively filling the **rocket box** to the rim with brown, mushy matter. After he had spread out the entire contents of the brownie bag, he stood back to admire his handiwork—a brimming can of caca. He smiled to himself, replaced the lid, picked up the heavy box, and walked back down the trail toward camp, practicing his best angry looks.

While he had been frosting the tops of the poo pods, his fellow guide had organized the guests and had gotten them into the **paddle raft**, which was parked next to the **gear raft** on the beach. He would be guiding the paddle raft that day and was sitting in the stern, telling the guests what rapids, hikes, hot springs, and pictographs they would be stopping to enjoy that day. He had finished tying the load on the gear raft, and now the only thing that needed to be tied on was the groover.

Brownie Guide entered the scene, inwardly brimming with anticipation and glee but effectively playing the part of the angry, disgruntled guide forced to break down the groover. There was a bad feeling in the air as he approached the group sitting in the paddle raft. The guests fell silent as he neared their raft, stopping two feet off the bow.

The guides' eyes locked in silence. There was tension on the beach.

"Took you long enough! We've gotta make miles today! Tie that on and let's go."

"I broke the damned thing down. Get off my back, you Nazi!"

The guest's heads wagged back and forth as if they were watching a tennis match.

"That's it, I'm gonna call to have you flown out at Mackay Bar. You need to take some time off. I'm sick of working with you."

"Well, I'm tired of working with *you*!" said Brownie Guide, dropping the rocket box in the sand with a thud.

"Careful with that, you dork! It could pop open. Then you'd have a mess to clean up."

Brownie Guide sucked in a deep breath and screamed, red-faced and furious, "NO I WON'T! *YOU WILL!!!*", then popped off the lid and reached into the slick mass of sticky brown slime.

An audible gasp came from the guests. Eight pairs of eyes watched in silent, breathless horror as Brownie Guide raised a handful of "turds" above his head and brandished it menacingly.

"*NOTHING TO SAY NOW, HUH, SMART GUY!!?*"

"Just take it easy. Put that down. You're not being rational," said the other guide, who seemed suddenly less willing to spar with Brownie Guide.

"PISS OFF!!!!"

And with that, to the horror of the guests sitting helplessly between the two guides, a volley of brown slime was launched, followed by another and another—"poo" rained down on them in thick, sticky chunks. All the guests in the paddle boat dove into the river to escape the onslaught, leaving the two guides convulsing with laughter, gasping for air and holding their stomachs. Actually, it was hardly laughter at all—more like sadistic cackling.

The first guest to emerge cautiously from the safety of the water reportedly witnessed both guides licking their fingers and having the following conversation:

"I like the walnuts in here."

"Me too."

She immediately resubmerged.

5

Mirage of Poo

Groover Type: *Classic Without Bags*
Rating:

This classic groover tale was told to me by Steve Cutright, a river guide from the days of yore who is now a fire chief someplace in the Bay Area and a responsible family man. He actually interviewed me for my first job as a raft guide back in 1986 and had the good sense to hire me.

Steve has been running rivers since the early seventies and has many stories to tell about wild runs through monstrous rapids, rain storms that last for weeks at a time, commissary boxes without utensils, food boxes without coffee, and many other predicaments, large and small. Steve is also a fine source of groover stories. He's seen a lot of shit. This is a tale he shared with me about an unfortunate sequence of events during a particularly long and blisteringly hot **shuttle** after a lengthy Grand Canyon river trip. I want to remind you that this is a *true* story and is not the product of my imagination, although I wish it were.

A hot wind blasted into the cab and dried out the already dry faces of the two young men slouching and blinking on the vinyl seats of the old Ford. They breathed slowly and carefully for fear of scorching their nostrils, as it was a particularly hot afternoon. For a while they had attempted conversation but it soon became clear that it was too hot to talk. They sat in silence and drove, sipping from the cans of tepid beer that rested between their legs as they watched the scrub brush and saguaro cactus roll by.

It had been one of the best trips that either of them had ever been on: much laughing, plenty of beer, a few layover days at amazing camps, and many hours spent pushing on oars and marveling at the beauty of Grand Canyon. They were deeply tanned and sporting scruffy beards from eighteen days of avoiding razors. The showers they had taken at the Big 6 motel had scrubbed away much of the trip's grime, but remnants of Colorado River silt remained in their sunbleached hair and in their ears and noses as well. They wore dingy T-shirts, faded nylon shorts, and river sandals—as well as sunglasses and visors to keep the glare down as it reflected off route 93 and into the hot cab of the truck.

Just after they had driven across the great plug of Hoover Dam and begun heading up the winding switchbacks out of the canyon of the murdered Colorado, the truck overheated, shooting plumes of white steam out from beneath its hood. The driver swore and slammed on the brakes. He stepped out into the baking heat to lift the hood and waited for the steam to clear, then stuffed a rag neatly in the newly formed hole. After filling the radiator up with a gallon of water from behind the seat, he got back in and slammed the door, and they continued the slow climb out of the canyon.

They emerged onto the high plateau. The road stretched out in front of them and the truck picked up speed. After eighteen days of moving at floating and hiking speeds, sixty-five miles per hour was a little unsettling and both of them felt a longing to return to the simple life they had enjoyed in Grand Canyon: floating amongst the million-year-old rocks, frolicking on the beaches, and exploring the labyrinthine side canyons. By comparison, the "real" world felt difficult to deal with: their stop at the convenience store in Las Vegas was almost as daunting as running Lava Falls, and they got their gas and a twelve-pack of cheap beer and retreated to the truck, escaping onto the interstate as quickly as they could.

The truck was a stout outfit: a 1972 Ford F250 four-wheel-drive, painted cream and brown—it looked sort of like a rusty root beer float as it bombed along through the desert heat. It was terribly overloaded with rafts, oars, life-jackets, **ammo cans**, food boxes, and, of course, the groovers. There were three of them tied together at the top of the pile, proudly riding in the position of prominence high above the rest of the jangle and jumble of faded river gear. The **hoopie** tying the boxes to each other and to the truck's rack was a tad old and faded. It was actually quite thin in one spot, and under considerable pressure where it rubbed against the metal rack.

Sitting high and mighty in the hot sun, the rocket boxes were under the constant bombardment of those incessant rays. These groovers also had no garbage bag **pods** containing the turds, as this was a bagless system. They had in them only the **goodness** and nothing more—three cans of raw sewage cooking in the Arizona sun.

The truck blasted along through the midday heat.

The men sipped their cheap beers and stared off into the shimmering, sparse landscape, their dark brown arms resting on the hot door metal.

The faded hoopie flapped along under tension at the point where it rubbed against the truck's rack. The cumulative ultraviolet damage to its fibers had caused it to fray almost imperceptibly. It began to unravel.

They drove along in silence behind their sunglasses, wishing that the air conditioning had not broken almost three weeks before on the way to the put-in.

A corner was coming up, so the fellow driving applied the brakes and slowed the forward motion of the over-loaded outfit. As he eased into the corner and accelerated out of it, something caught his eye in the rearview mirror. At the same moment, both of them heard a heavy thud and metallic scraping.

"What the . . . ?"

"Pull over, man. What the hell just flew off?"

They stopped the truck, got out, and looked back down the road to the corner they had just come around. They couldn't see much out of the ordinary—just a heat mirage like they had been seeing all day, and three square boxes lying in the road.

"Oh no. Are those our groovers?"

"No."

"Oh, man, they are. Look, they're not up there," said one of them, pointing to the rack. "That **hoopie** broke. Those are the groovers and that mirage is no mirage. That's a mirage of poo."

The two of them stood there in the sun looking out from beneath their visors at the even coating of turds that lay across the entire width of Route 93.

"What should we do?"

One of them slowly scratched his head. This was a significant problem. It seemed like some kind of bad dream—a hallucination inspired by the heat, the driving, and the cheap, warm beer.

As they stood pondering the poo puddle, three bicycle tourists suddenly rounded the corner, haplessly peddling straight toward the spill. They stood and watched in disbelief, powerless to help three fellow humans drifting toward what they thought was just another fake lake in the road: They knew their warning screams would not be heard until it was too late.

The first cyclist went completely through the slick, the foul and fetid slime spinning up onto his Oakley sunglasses and splattering up the back of his Campagnolo jersey. He uttered a warning yell to his fellow riders, but not soon enough. The second rider had already entered the first half of the turd zone and was now frantically braking, trying to keep from soiling his spandex as his friend had done already. This applying of the brakes proved to be a bad idea, however, as it caused him to go into an uncontrolled skid. He went down onto the road and rolled around in the goodness—effectively covering himself from head to toe like a piece of shake-and-bake chicken. He began to try and get up, but slipped and fell back into the nasties repeatedly.

The third cyclist was luckiest of all; for he, after seeing what befell his two companions, applied his brakes in a timely fashion, stopping just on the border of the shit slick. All three of them looked down the road and saw the two rafters standing there in their shorts, sunglasses, and sandals, drinking their cheap beers. Their eyes locked and for a moment there was motionless silence. The wind blew a small tumbleweed across the road and they could hear its faint scratching.

The beer cans hit the ground simultaneously. The doors to the truck slammed and the tires squealed as it sped away from the scene, racing through the gears as it rounded the next bend. The cyclists remained there in the scorching heat of the sun, one of them marinating on the dotted line.

6

The Groover
That Ate Sonora

Groover Type: *Millennium Falcon*
Rating: 🧻🧻🧻🧻🧻

This is the grandmother of all groover stories. Actually, it is from this tale that the nasty idea for this book sprung. It was the first groover story I ever heard, and so I feel a certain connection to it. In fact, it has taken me a while to get to a point where I feel worthy of committing this one to the page. I hope that I have done it justice.

"The Groover That Ate Sonora" is a classic—the *Iliad* of the fecal genre, if you will. It was first told to me by Andy Anderson, who was a significant influence in my river guiding career, teaching me the intricacies of getting rafts down rivers with style and making perfect cakes in Dutch ovens, among other things. He looks like a scaled-down version of Grizzly Adams and, like Grizzly, spent much of his life in the outdoors, most of it as a wilderness guide leading groups of youths (the troubled kind) into the wilds of the Southwest. He is an interesting person. Last I heard he was selling insurance in Ukiah, California.

Andy told me this over a pitcher of beer one evening at a guide hangout on the South Fork of the American River in California where I drank many an underaged beer as a neophyte river guide. He took a sip from his glass, cleared some foam off his mustache with thumb and forefinger, looked at me with his piercing blue eyes, and began to recount the events of that hot summer day in Sonora, California.

Gear was spread out everywhere on the Ward's Ferry Bridge—take-out for the Tuolumne River, just outside the small town of Sonora in the Sierra foothills. There were piles of life vests, stacks of coolers, and bags of leftover beer and soda, all cooking in the slanting afternoon sunlight. The crew of guides scurried about the bridge in their river sandals and shorts, organizing the gear and loading the truck.

She was a 1972 International crew cab, painted like an Avon raft—gray with a yellow stripe around her middle. The gray paint looked a lot like primer and was rusting through in a few spots, giving her sort of an unkempt look. The leaf springs on one side were shot and so she listed a tad to the left. She had been in the Outdoor Adventures fleet for many years and would see several more seasons after this one. She was a hard-working truck, and was well-loved by the guides who drove her; she was kind of ugly, but strong and functional. She also provided a true test of one's ability to drive a manual transmission: one of her many idiosyncrasies was a habit of throwing the gear shift out of third and into the naked knee of the person driving.

The crew of six guides frantically climbed all over the truck to load her, tying frames, oars, and piles of life vests on top of her, and tightly rolled 150-pound rafts in her bed, followed by a jumble of military **ammo cans**, **rocket boxes**, coolers, water bottles, boat pumps, commissary boxes, and empty beer cans. Slowly she began to settle down on her springs and into the ground.

It had been a fine river trip and the guides were in high spirits as they worked. The tower of gear in the truck bed and resting on the rusty rack atop the crew cab grew and grew. When at last they were almost finished, the load looked like the multicolored hat that a character would wear in a Dr. Seuss book. The truck was now listing noticeably to the port side.

The load was not complete though. The groover had been saved for last and now the time had come to tie it on. The easiest spot to do so was on the top of the pile of life vests that were piled on top of the six **oar frames** which sat heavily on the rack above the cab. One of the guides volunteered and climbed to the top of the load, a piece of **hoopie** in hand, ready to lash the groover to the top of the teetering load like the star atop a Christmas tree. Two other guides carefully passed the brimming Millennium Falcon-style groover up.

As you remember from chapter one, "Types of Groovers," the Millennium Falcon consists of a flat plastic tank about six inches high and two and a half feet square. A toilet seat insert fits into the top of the tank, right over a hole that is opened by pressing on a pedal on the side of the tank. The intention of this system is to use gravity to whisk turds down and into the plastic tank, through the open hole. But an open hole is an open hole. Items can go in and items can come out.

Not wanting to have any movement or potential leakage of the fetid poo stew that lurked within the tank, the guide on the top of the load tied that tank down well, using **trucker's hitch** knots and a crisscross pattern that secured it firmly in place. What he did not notice as he tied that last knot was that one of the taut lines rested only a half-inch above the pedal.

"Looks good. Let's go!" He climbed down from his perch.

All six guides crammed into the cab, three in front and three in back. The International made its final settle into its springs. The driver turned the key that dangled loosely in the ignition. With a roar, a few gasps and wheezes, and a plume of blue smoke, the International pulled off the bridge and up the steep, winding hill to Sonora. As the rig made the first corner, a **bail bucket** moved, almost imperceptibly in the bed of the truck and the load shifted. Just a tiny bit. About a half-inch.

The winding roadway out of the Tuolumne canyon was sticky with heat, and all the windows were rolled down to get some breeze blowing through the cab. It had been a three-day trip in severe heat, and even though the river was wonderful to rinse off and cool down in, none of them had really taken baths, and with all six crammed into the cab that afternoon, the breeze was needed for more than temperature regulation. They were a tad ripe.

The truck teetered around a sharp switchback and an **ammo can** fell onto its side. The load shifted once more.

It is not a short drive from Ward's Ferry to Sonora, but it is a pretty one, through golden, folding hills peppered with dark green oak trees. The International roared by small farms with cows munching in the shade of large trees, taking a rest from the sun that roasted the grass in the pastures. As the guides bounced along these back roads they told stories about river trips and had many laughs. It was a fine afternoon.

Just on the outskirts of town a jackrabbit darted out in front of the International's front tires. "Jesus!" exclaimed the driver, slamming on the brakes as the rabbit skittered nervously into the tall grass on the side of the road. The guides felt their seat belts bite into their stomachs as they slid forward on the vinyl seats. This time they could hear and feel the contents of the overloaded International moving forward, **ammo cans** clanging as the truck surged up on its front wheels.

"I think you missed him."

"Almost killed us."

And they drove on toward what they thought would be a routine breakdown of trip gear: putting things back in the warehouse, washing out coolers, and drinking beer.

Unbeknownst to them, a frightening fecal drama was unfolding six feet above their heads in the crown of the load that swayed in the hot wind. . . .

The initial shifts in the gear pyramid while they were driving out of the river canyon had moved the load enough so that the line of hoopie that had been hovering a half-inch above the groover's pedal came to rest firmly on top of it. When they hit the brakes to avoid the jackrabbit, the groover, along with the rest of the tower of gear, had surged forward five to six inches, forcing the pedal into the taut line and opening the tank to the outside world. At the same moment that the trap door opened, the tank tilted up and forward, getting wedged on its side. The liquefied soup of poo then began to pour steadily out of the tank and onto the bundles of life vests that rested beneath it.

Meanwhile, in the cab, the guides continued talking, laughing, and telling stories. It had gotten even hotter and many of them had taken their shirts off, riding along with sweaty backs sticking to vinyl seats, arms out windows, and a breeze blowing through the cab. They had entered Sonora and were coming to the first stoplight they'd seen in four days. The driver applied the brakes and the load shifted again just slightly.

The foul mixture was slowly crawling toward the unsuspecting guides in the cab below. It had percolated through the bundles of life vests, fouled the oars beneath, and was now dripping onto the top of the cab, spreading out in a wandering, soupy puddle. The stop at the light had tilted the tank still more and a new surge of effluent began to leak down through the load.

They sat at the stoplight, waiting for it to change. A single drop of fluid hung from the top of the driver's side door unnoticed, glinting in the sun.

"What's that smell?"

"Yick. I dunno. Man! It's awful."

The drop fell silently through the air and landed warmly on the driver's arm. At the same moment, a consistent stream began to spatter on the arm of the passenger-side guide; then more trickles and rivulets appeared on the driver's side and in the back windows as well.

"OH, MY GOD! THE GROOVER!!!"

They frantically rolled all the windows up, hands slipping off the handles in their zeal to escape the unyielding tide of liquefied turds that pursued them.

The light turned green.

The honking of the cars behind them jolted them from their living nightmare and the driver pulled slowly through the intersection, the goodness still streaming down the side windows.

They all sat crammed together in that reeking cell, their bare backs and thighs sticking to the seats, the temperature rising, a mixture of sweat and feces on their arms, some with splatters in their beards—all held prisoner by that which streamed down the windows. No one spoke. They were just trying not to vomit.

It came down the windshield.

They had no choice.

"Hit the wipers."

The mixture smeared out on the glass in front of them as they raced through the streets of Sonora, tires screeching around corners, the teetering load now looking as if it would fall off any second. The scene was shocking to the innocent citizens of Sonora: six horror-stricken pale-faced young men behind turd-stained glass rocketing recklessly through the streets of their town.

At one point a Sonora city policeman raced up next to the International with his lights blazing and a stern glower on his face, but when he saw and smelled what was flowing down the cab he waved the truck on and hit his brakes to escape the oppressive smell.

The truck barreled into a car wash stall and the driver turned off the engine. The streams continued to flow down the windows in steady rivulets.

"Someone has to get out and wash it off," said the driver.

No one said a word.

"Who's gonna get out and turn on the hose?"

Nothing.

"Crap!" he said, drawing in a reluctant breath and trying not to gag. He opened his door quickly, drips and globs landing on his back as he sprinted for the hose, desperately fumbling for quarters. The others sat sweating in the fouled cab and waited to be rescued by the cleansing waters of the hose. They were finally safe.

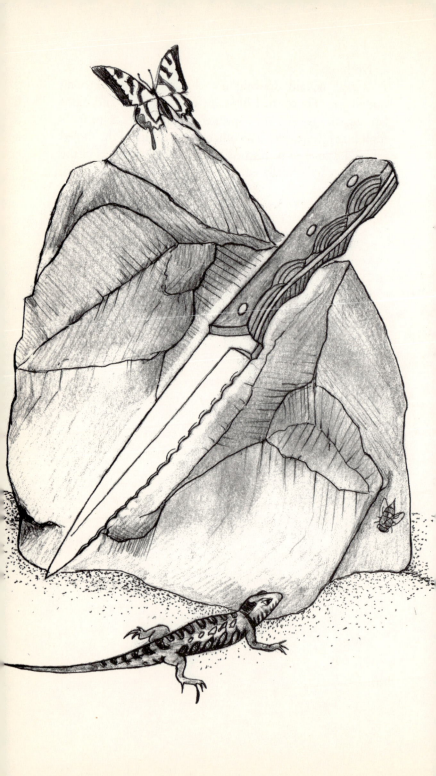

7

The Knife

Groover Type: *Classic with Bags*
Rating: 🗑️ 🗑️ 🗑️

In order to cook and prepare the amazing meals that are a part of most river trips these days, river guides must bring along on their rafts a complete kitchen with all of the tools and utensils needed to work culinary magic for the guests. All of the bowls, plates, pots, and pans are stored in a large, waterproof container made of metal, called the **commissary** or "comm" box. The guides haul this large rusting object up and down rocky river banks, trying not to take chunks out of their shins.

In this box there is a smaller box where all of the utensils are kept. Unlike most home utensil sets, which match nicely, the flatware in a river commissary is a random, mismatched collection of forks, spoons, and knives jangling around in a dingy Tupperware container.

Often, as I've sifted through that eclectic collection of forks, knives, and spoons, I've wondered about the stories that were there. Here is a particularly nasty tale about a steak knife that did some dirty deeds on California's Tuolumne River.

35

Kim wasn't comfortable with the groover. She never had been. She couldn't believe that the other guides actually *enjoyed* talking about it—they would even discuss the topic while they prepared food and while they ate. Just the idea of it made her feel nauseous. She knew that B.M.s were a part of life, but she didn't want to spend time *talking* about them. It seemed to her a sophomoric, adolescent thing to do.

Kim was an accountant from Orange County; she had taken up guiding to get herself out of the office a few weekends a summer. She liked the wildness of the river and she liked the other guides. They were fun people, but sometimes she just didn't feel like she related to them very well. They were, well, different than her, that was all.

One day, Kim sat stiffly on the seat of the groover, refusing to breathe through her nose as she moved her bowels. She looked straight ahead at the mighty Tuolumne as it slid by, a thick green band of cool water. Just downstream the river disappeared over the horizon line that was the beginning of Clavey Falls, one of the biggest rapids on the river. To take her mind off of what she was doing, she began to think about the chicken cordon bleu that she and the other guides would make for dinner that night.

She had organized this particular trip for her friends and wanted it to be perfect. Bob, Sherry, Nadine, Liz, Cyndi, and Richard were from the office, and Dale and Bill were from the club. They would get together once or twice a year, drink too much white wine, get silly, and play board games that they had given each other for Christmas. So far it seemed that everyone was having a good time on the trip. Kim had planned the menu and had spent hours putting the recipes together for the delicate hors d'oeuvres, sumptuous main courses, and surprisingly complex desserts that impressed her friends to no end. This pleased Kim—much more than sitting on that foul metal box making a number two.

"There, that's done," she said to herself once she was finished. She raised her shorts into place and shut the lid quickly so that no smell or sight would escape, then carefully placed the toilet paper back on the rock next to the groover. She breathed a sigh of relief and decided to go pick some lupines that were growing in purple bursts just down the trail and stick them into a woodpecker hole in the oak tree next to the groover. When the flowers were in place she stood back to admire her handiwork. Very nice.

As she turned to go, something caught her eye. Sitting on a rock five feet away from the box was a steak knife—just like the ones that were in the commissary box down in camp: a brown, plastic handle with a thin, serrated blade. *That's silly*, she thought. *What was somebody doing bringing one of our knives up here?* She picked it up gingerly and made her way down to camp.

Now, the classic groover with bags, like the one that Kim had been using, produces, as you know, a foul fruit—the plastic turd **pod**. When dumping this type of groover at the end of trips, guides are faced with a significant ethical dilemma: how are they to *dispose* of the pods?

For many, the answer is to throw them covertly into landfills or even into dumpsters in the business districts of small, rural towns near river **take-outs**. I remember hiding one night under a blue tarp in the bed of a wheezing, 1973 Chevy crew cab, waiting for the signal from Tom, who was driving. He cut the engine and killed the lights. The truck coasted with only the crunching whisper of its tires down the narrow, dark alley behind a liquor store in Sonora, California.

"OK, Joe, *NOW!*"

And I threw back the tarp, reached into the open rocket box, and heaved three bulging, glistening garbage bags through the darkness. They landed on their mark, hitting the floor of the dumpster with resonating thuds. I hid beneath the tarp once again. Tom started the engine and turned on the lights, and we made our way out of town, both of us trying not to think of the sanitation worker who would be making his rounds the following week.

This same drill has also been executed less covertly. I once heard of a small group of commercial guides who were seen cheering and singing like gleeful school children, "Pods in the dumpster, pods in the dumpster," as they arced foul, weighty orbs into a Forest Service can on the side of a busy highway. Shameless.

But there is another, more responsible way to deal with these pods. It is not for the faint of heart or weak of stomach. It is a hands-on, high-exposure duty, and it is the method that the guides on the Tuolumne had been using the season that Kim was picking lupines and putting them in the woodpecker holes in the oak tree next to the groover.

The high-exposure plastic pod disposal procedure goes like this: First a guide is chosen—usually through a "rosham-bo" or "rock, paper, scissors" contest. He or she takes the groover to a "green dome"-style portable toilet (the kind you see at construction sites and rock concerts). The guide then puts on some surgical gloves and sunglasses, props open the door to the green dome, and pops off the groover's lid. Then she reaches into the groover and removes one pendulous, moist bag of poo, quickly bringing it into the green dome, and holding it above the hole into which construction workers and concert-goers relieve themselves. Then she takes a knife, pierces the bag, retracts her hand immediately, and squeezes the bulging bag like a baker decorating a birthday cake, directing the stream of liquefied human waste into the hole.

They repeat this process until all of the bags have been popped and drained of their contents. The soiled bags are then thrown into a dumpster, as are the surgical gloves since they have usually sustained some splatters. It is, in all, a nasty job.

As you can see, integral to this process is a well-sharpened knife that cuts through plastic quickly and smoothly, allowing the guide to retract his or her gloved hand with a minimal amount of hand-to-shit contact. This knife is placed in the groover, and all guides understand that it will always remain there. It will be used for one thing and one thing only—lancing shit bags.

Back at the fateful campsite, all of the guides were standing behind the long serving tables wearing their aprons and drinking gin and tonics as the early evening shadows stretched up the canyon of the mighty Tuolumne. (The gin and tonic was the official drink of Tuolumne guides.) The guests sat on rocks and **ammo cans** in a quiet circle next to the river, hunched over their plates in their laps, busily chewing and savoring each bite of the fantastic meal. Most of them had spent a long day hiking up the wild and scenic Clavey River, exploring and swimming in its many pools. They were hungry.

Under the careful eye and specific instructions of Kim, the guides had presented one of the most impressive meals that any of them had ever seen: roasted garlic, baked brie with raspberries, and roma tomatoes with fresh basil and olive oil for hors d'oeuvre, chicken cordon bleu, Caesar salad, wild rice, broccoli with garlic sauce, and French bread for the main course; fruit flambé for dessert—an impressive menu, indeed. Kim's friends were in heaven as they ate their food, slicing off pieces of chicken and poking them in their mouths, rolling their eyes and smacking their lips with delight; this made Kim feel wonderful.

One of the guides, Kirk, was up at the groover and he came down the trail looking a little pale and worried.

"You guys?" he said quietly once he was closer to the serving table and out of earshot of the guests.

"Yeah, Kirk. What's up, man? You don't look so good."

"Well, I was just up there at the groover."

"Yeah."

"Well, the knife's gone," he said, looking from side to side. "I couldn't find the knife up there."

"You mean the shit knife?"

"Yeah man, the shit knife," he said in a strained whisper. "The one we use to cut open the pods. It's not up there."

"It's gotta be up there. I put it on a rock just off to the side a little bit."

Kim's eyes had gotten quite large and she swallowed hard, looking out at the many knives that were resting on her friends' plates or slicing through the creamy pieces of chicken cordon bleu. All those knives had brown, plastic handles and thin, serrated blades. Kim reflected with horror on the serrations in such blades: little nooks and crannies that would collect bits of food—tiny crusties that you sometimes couldn't even scrub out with a sponge in the dish line.

"Wha . . . what did it look like, you guys?" she asked meekly.

"You mean the knife?"

"Yeah. What did it look like?"

"It was a steak knife, just like the ones we have in the utensil box. Just like the ones they're using now," said Kirk, gesturing over toward the contented guests.

"Oh no. Oh jeeze. Oh gosh you guys. I don't feel so good," said Kim and she went over to lean up against the house-sized granite boulder that created the kitchen nook where they had their stoves and tables set up.

"You guys, I brought the knife down here and put it in the dish line."

The other guides looked at her with fear in their eyes, their mouths hanging open slightly.

"I thought someone had forgotten it up there. I was just trying to tidy up a little. I didn't know. I didn't. Really."

They all slowly turned to see that, indeed, every knife had been set out and was now being used. Over there by the river, sitting on one of the customers' plates, was a knife that had been used countless times to slash open reeking bags of caca.

Kim began to cry quietly.

Kirk flashed his crooked teeth in a demonic grin and said, "Anyone for the chicken tonight?"

8

The Day the Mormon Swore

Groover Type: *Classic Without Bags*
Rating:

In doing my research for this book, I came across many tales of this nature. They were all quite vile but this one tickled my fancy a little more than the others because of a few unique details. It is truly a horrifying tale: read on only if you feel you are prepared for six rolls of nastiness.

Denny was a Mormon. He was no Jack Mormon either, he was the real McCoy. It was said that for as long as anyone could remember, Denny had never sworn at or insulted any*thing* or any*body*. He just wasn't that kind of guy. He'd say, "oh gosh," or "shucks," and things like that but would never let loose with any of the more base, commonly-used expletives. Those were not for him. He was good. The kind of guy who would ask, "How are you?" and really want to know. A genuinely nice guy.

Denny was clean, too, and good looking—tall and strong, with blue eyes that glinted in the sun beneath his river hat. He had straight, strong, blindingly white teeth. His dad owned the rafting company where Denny was the general manager and he had grown up on the river—had been guiding rafts since he was a teenager. He loved rafting and the culture that surrounded it, although there were times at river guide gatherings when he would become uncomfortable, what with all of the drinking and polluting of temples that was going on around him. He didn't let that get between him and his buddies, though. They were just different from him. He loved them and never said a bad thing nor, as far as anyone could gather, thought a bad thought, about any of them.

He was pure and strong and kind. He wore pastel polo shirts, which he tucked into his shorts. His hair was always short and stubble was never seen upon his face. That was Denny, and everybody loved him.

May 27, 1988

Mike and Bucky had been working in the rain for about an hour, unloading the wet gear from a three-day, early spring trip on the Forks of the Kern. They scurried back and forth from the bed of the rusting white 1968 Dodge Power Wagon to the dry, cavernous warehouse echoing with the ping of raindrops. They wore hooded rain jackets, ratty blue jeans, and hiking boots that tracked mud onto the warehouse's smooth cement floor.

It had rained for the last three days with no breaks. The river had been high and runnable, but the constant rain had taken its toll on both of them. Neither had been dry for seventy-two hours and they looked forward to warm showers, dry clothes, and a few rounds of shuffleboard and beers at the Shady Lane Saloon, the local guide hangout.

Bucky had trained on the trip, rowing his own raft and learning as much as he could about the river when he wasn't flailing down it. He had provided many hours of entertainment as well as plenty of emergency rescue practice for the other members of the crew. He wrapped his raft around granite boulders in the middle of large class V rapids three separate times and flipped twice.

The waterproof bags that season were old and leaky, so many of the guests never wore dry clothes or slept in dry sleeping bags for the whole three days. Things had worked out though. The guides had built large fires, brewed a lot of coffee and cocoa, and set up ingenious tarp contraptions that sheltered everyone from the rain; so the trip had actually been quite enjoyable.

Then, on the last night, Glenn, one of the guides, discovered that there was no meat for the night's dinner. Somehow the chicken had been forgotten. All they had was rice, bread, vegetables for a salad, and a few other random food items banging around in the bottom of the coolers. After a few moments brainstorming and taking inventory of his larders, Glenn decided that he would steal the sausage from the next morning's breakfast and use the rice, veggies and an assortment of herbs and spices to create "rice-sausage surprise." The result was a big, big hit and apparently a few of the guests asked Glenn for his recipe. It was a fine bit of improvising.

The rain continued to plink steadily onto the sheet metal roof of the warehouse. Bucky was now in the bed of the Power Wagon, handing **rocket boxes** and coolers down to Mike. "Hey Mike, you're trip leader. You have to deal with the groover," he said joyfully as he handed down the heavy rocket box with "groover" stenciled across its lid in blue lettering.

"I know, Bucky. I'll just put it here by the fence for now and we'll deal with it as soon as we get everything else done," Mike said as he set the box down carefully next to the chain-link fence. It had been a full trip—fifteen people. Three days. Lots of turds in that box.

"You mean *you'll* deal with it."

"Yeah, right, Bucky, *I'll* deal with it."

In many commercial rafting companies it is an unwritten rule that the lead guide is responsible for the dumping and cleaning of the groover. Mike knew that this was his duty and he had every intention of doing it but he also had a lot of other things on his mind that cold and rainy afternoon—things like dryness, shuffleboard, beer, and Patsy Cline playing on the jukebox.

They worked hard and quietly for another thirty minutes, washing coolers, folding sandy tarps, hanging up wetsuits, and placing frames and oars in their designated spots. Finally, they were finished.

"Good job, Buck. Let's get back to the house and take those showers. I could use one."

"Yeah you could," said Bucky, "I've been smelling your **polypro** for the last three days. Nasty!"

"Shut up and get in the truck, you rookie," said Mike jokingly as he pulled the driver's side door shut with a creak of its hinges. Bucky eagerly jumped into the passenger side and slammed his door. He was full of the enthusiasm of a young guide and he liked hanging around with Mike—just like one of the guys. Mike was a great guide and Bucky respected him.

As they drove out of the warehouse parking lot, leaving track marks in the thin brown mud, neither noticed the rocket box with the blue stenciled letters still sitting heavily and quietly by the chain-link fence.

That night Bucky and Mike had a great time at the Shady Lane—shuffleboard, beer, Patsy, and many gnarly river stories. Mike woke up early the next morning; he had to work an eighty-day Outward Bound backpacking course and needed to get up to Oregon by the next day for his pre-trip meeting with the other instructors. After he had organized the duffel bags of clothes and milk crates of food and books in the back of his green 1968 V.W. squareback, he pulled out of the guide house driveway, trying not to spill the coffee which he held between his legs, and drove down highway 178 into the glare of the early spring sunshine. He would not return to the Kern Valley until September.

As Mike was putting on his shades, kicking off his river sandals, and placing his left foot on the dash, a powerful gust of wind blew through the Kern Valley. Mike felt it push the square green car that he called "Zuke" slightly to the right, but he easily corrected and continued down the highway. Back in the warehouse parking lot, a piece of rotting, spongy plywood that was leaning against the chain-link caught that blast of wind and fell sideways, slicing through the air. Its edge fell solidly into the moist mud in front of the forgotten groover.

A light rain began to fall in the valley. Mike turned on his wipers, took off his shades, and turned the volume up. He liked this song.

August 15, 1988

The valley was like an oven, even early in the morning. It was seven o'clock and only a few shreds of shade were left in the dusty warehouse parking lot. The area was littered with the peculiar things that collect in such places: the rusting hulk of a 1964 Mercedes sedan, thirty salvaged toilets with weeds sprouting from their orifices, discarded garden hoses, beer cans, broken-down belt sanders, an old bus parked in the weeds on the far side, broken oars, tattered life vests, old scraps of rotting lumber—all of it covered with a fine coat of the brown dust that whirled around the lot in frantic, angry funnels. The average high temperature that summer was 97 degrees.

Denny swallowed hard and pulled the visor of his baseball cap down to shade his cracking lips. His blue eyes were squinting into the hot, dirty wind as he walked through the lot. He didn't have a whole lot on his schedule that day since it was late in the season and business was slowing down. It had been a great summer. They had run many trips and had even made a little money—which was a rarity in the outfitting business. He was out for a walk around the warehouse, checking things out—just poking around.

Denny had never really liked all of the old, worthless stuff that his dad collected. It seemed useless to him to hold onto things just because they might need them someday. He knew, for instance, that they would never use all those toilets. Why did they keep them? *Sheesh*, he thought to himself, *it seems so darn silly.*

He saw a piece of dry and flaking plywood leaning against the chain-link fence. His dad probably wanted to save this to make some gear decks out of—which was ridiculous because that wood was plain rotten and couldn't be used for anything—anyone could see that. Denny reached out and grabbed the sheet of wood irritably and jerked it back.

The early morning sun shone down on the rocket box for the first time in three and a half months. Denny could not see the blue stenciled letters because they were covered with dust.

"Hmmm," he said, as he studied the box.

The sides of the can were bulging outward. The lid had curved and was slightly warped, a tight and shiny metal skin. Denny crouched to get a better look at the box, his light blue polo shirt coming untucked from his shorts. Had the light been better or had he been thinking more clearly, perhaps he would not have reached toward the release mechanism on the clamp closest to him.

He says now that his hand didn't even touch the lever, but that once it was close enough merely the agitation of the air molecules was enough of a disruption to detonate that festering, well-seasoned turd bomb.

The big-haired ladies gossiping in the realty office across the street heard the dull thud of the explosion and they fell silent.

Denny can't remember what he heard. He actually doesn't remember much of anything from those first few seconds, but my exhaustive research suggests the following sequence of events:

When Denny touched the clamp, the lid flew up with a deafening blast. Since its other side was still attached to the box, the lid jammed open at an angle. At that instant, a thundering geyser of liquefied, superheated, three-month-old shit slammed into the angled underside of the lid and ricocheted squarely into Denny's face. His head snapped back from the force and he was knocked to the ground and sent sprawling in the dust of the parking lot, his entire upper body and head covered in the vile mixture. He sat silently in disbelief, the explosion still ringing in his ears. The box then continued to anoint him with a fine, reeking mist as the lid bobbed up and down like a hellish Pac-Man. He blinked twice and then began to do something he had never done before—he said some bad words.

The ladies in the realty office say that they had never heard such horrible language. They say that he went through every word in the book that morning but his favorite was the "s" word, which he just kept saying over and over as he wiped his eyes and stumbled through that strange collection of old toilets that his dad was saving.

9

Mask of Poo

Groover Type: *Classic with Bags*
Rating: 🧻🧻🧻🧻🧻

This classic story, like "Turd Sandwich," details a misadventure that many river guides have had bad dreams about but very few have actually experienced. It was told to me by one of its two characters, Heidi White, a river guide of great skill and a wonderful human being with a terrific enthusiasm for rivers and people. She has a smile that endears her to most who meet her, and she is a wonderful and energetic spinner of yarn. As you can see by the rating, this one is kind of nasty.

The trip had been wonderful, and the weather hot and clear for the entire six days. The boat ramp at Vinegar Creek, **take-out** for Idaho's Main Salmon River, was cooking in the late morning sun and gear was sprawled out all over the place in multicolored piles. The crew of ten guides cleaned coolers, organized the back of the truck, passed oars up to the rack to be tied on, and rolled big, slimy rafts. It had been a private, all-guide trip, and so the work was getting done quickly—even though some people were moving

51

kind of slowly due to the libations they had consumed the previous night.

"Who wants to help me deal with the groover?"

"I suppose I will, Heidi," replied Jed.

"Could be kinda gross, Jed. You sure?"

"Yeah. No problem."

Jed was a little squeamish about the groover—in his years as a guide, he had never really warmed up to the whole idea of crapping in a box. Heidi gave him the opportunity to back away from the groover that day but he would have none of it. As it turned out, he should have taken the out that Heidi offered.

Bending down to grab one of the handles of the can, Heidi said, "All right, Jed, grab the other handle and let's carry it up there."

At the time of the events of this story, the classic with bags was the most widely used groover. To deal with the problem of poop **pod** disposal, the rangers from the Nez Perce National Forest had designed a receptacle system which they employed at Vinegar Creek. This "system" was a big, brown, smelly dumpster into which river runners slung their pods of turds. For obvious reasons, it was up and away from the rest of the take-out area, on a small rise above the boat ramp.

Jed and Heidi trekked up the hill in the scorching August sun, their burden bending their backs.

"Heavy, huh, Jed?"

"Uh huh."

"Almost there."

The can they carried had five pods of poo and was almost completely full. They reached the dumpster and set the can down with a heavy thud, next to the foul brown box. Flies buzzed in their eyes and about their heads.

"OK, Jed, we need to do this quickly. I don't want to have the groover or that dumpster open any longer than is absolutely necessary."

"I know. Me neither."

"Here's what we'll do: First I'll open the dumpster and prop open the door. While I'm doing that you'll open the groover."

"Got it."

"Then I will reach into the groover and grab the first pod. As I am hoisting and slinging that pod into the dumpster, you will lean down and get the second pod. While you sling the second pod I will be grabbing the third, and so on. Timing is crucial. We must keep a steady and predictable rhythm going if we are to make this work."

"Yeah. Got it."

"You ready?" said Heidi, poised with her hand on the lid of the reeking dumpster.

"Yeah, go ahead."

Heidi opened the dumpster door with a grimace as the foul rotting stench leaked out. Jed opened the groover. Heidi reached for the first pod and slung while Jed reached for the second. Jed slung the second while Heidi reached for the third. All was going smoothly and according to plan. Heidi slung the third as Jed reached for the fourth.

But as Jed lifted that fourth pod of turds he realized it was not like all the others. It was heavier and more cumbersome. *Morning two,* he remembered, *rich breakfast.* That pod slowed him. His sling was not nearly as graceful as the others had been—in fact it looked for a second as though it might miss its mark and get snagged on one of the dumpster's sharp corners. Thankfully it made it and dropped solidly on target, but Jed was a little off balance now. He was, so to speak, not in the groove.

Just as Jed had regained his balance and was turning in a sweeping motion back toward the empty groover, Heidi was in the power sweep of the fifth pod sling. The pod whistled through the air with great speed. To Heidi and Jed's mutual horror, they saw that, because of his break in pod-slinging rhythm, the hurtling fifth orb of shit was on a collision course with Jed's face. Heidi's final swing had nowhere else to go.

Now, this pod had been sitting in the bottom of that groover for six days. Many of those days had been quite hot, so the poo had been given every opportunity to fester and ferment in there. A certain mysterious liquid often collects in the bottom of the groover by the sixth day, and the lower pods are often bathed in it. Optimists say, "Oh it's just a little river water that leaked in," but for those of us more bitterly grounded in reality, we know what that stuff really is: *poo juice*. This fifth bag was fairly shimmering with it as it accelerated towards Jed's face.

His mouth was open as if to scream, but he never had a chance to. The bag hit him with a solid slap and folded around his head, enveloping him in wet folds of foul-smelling brown plastic. Heidi said later that she was able to detect an imprint of Jed's face as it pressed into the plastic bag, forming a poo-pod mask that he wore for a split second. Of course, the ultimate horror would have been for the bag to break at this point, but thankfully its tensile strength was high. It held.

When the pod fell away, Heidi, who was still holding the swinging bag, stood looking into the saucer-sized eyes of her horrified friend.

"Oh my God, Jed. I'm so sorry. I'm sorry. Oh my God."

He closed his mouth and stifled a scream between lips he dared not reopen. A solitary drip of juice ran down the length of his nose and hung there on its end, tickling him for an instant before falling away.

Jed sprinted toward the green and winding river, some 100 yards away, covering the distance in record time, and frantically bathed himself for twenty minutes, screaming intermittently.

Heidi tossed the pod into the dumpster and closed its lid, sealed the groover and slowly made her way back down to the ramp, shaking her head.

"He shouldn't have done that. He broke rhythm."

10

Swirlies at His Ankles

Groover Type: *Jon–ny Partner*
Rating:

This, I am afraid, is another of the more disgusting groover tales and not one for the meek or tender of stomach. If you are not prepared for a five-roller, I encourage you to read no further. If you are prepared, and think yourself up to a tale of significant nastiness, please read on, as I find this to be a rather interesting (if vile) story. I have written it here as accurately as possible and indeed it is fairly true to fact; for I was actually present for this one—an actor in this fecal drama.

It was the last night of a trip on the Middle Fork of the Salmon; this means fiesta night—fajitas, margaritas, talent show by guests and guides, and general merry-making. It is usually the most festive night on the river, and is often followed by a little dehydration the next morning.

The section of canyon that we navigate that last day is one of the most spectacular I have ever had the pleasure of floating through in my many years of river-running. The walls are sheer and tower many hundreds of feet above the clear, swiftly moving river. The rapids are some of the most impressive of the trip: Rubber, Hancock, Devil's Tooth, House Rock, Jump Off, and several others. Of all of them, Rubber—a series of large, crashing waves—is the most impressive and has been responsible for many a flip and swimmer throughout the years.

On this particular morning, we were camped at Tumble Creek, often referred to as Stumble Creek due to the rather long, steep, and rocky trail that much of the gear must be carried up and down. It is also said that after a few margaritas on the last night, people tend to stumble around in this camp.

So there we were on the last morning—most of us tired, some of us dehydrated, and all of us thankful for the discovery of the coffee bean. We were efficiently packing up camp and getting the boats rigged, a task that by this point in the trip was second nature for guests and guides alike.

I was the lead guide, which means that, among other things, I was responsible for giving instructional talks to the guests at certain points during the trip. The talk on the last morning is to inform everyone of the routine once we hit the boat ramp at the **take-out**. "Blah, blah, blah," said I, and the guests all listened attentively. While I was giving this talk, Dave—a fellow guide who was rowing the gear boat that day—was breaking down the groover. It was of the Jon-ny Partner variety and so had a rubber drain plug in the side of its large cubic storage tank.

Dave was rowing a very large and very old raft from the 1970s. It was what we guides call a "bucket boat" or **non-self-bailing raft**. In such a craft, one must use a five-gallon plastic **bail bucket** to scoop the water out of the bilge after going through rapids. The more cutting-edge rafts of the '90s are self-bailing, with handy little holes along the sides of the inflatable floor out of which water flows effortlessly, thus leaving guests and guides free of the annoyance of bailing after rapids.

After adding some water to the turds to ensure quick and easy cleanup after the trip, sealing the lid, clamping down the clamp, carrying the Jon-ny down the rocky trail, and walking past the group of guests listening to my enthralling oratory on the virtues of quick take-outs, Dave placed the silver cube on his raft. He then loaded the boat with waterproof bags, **commissary boxes**, **ammo cans**, and bags of beer and soda.

At one point while I was giving my talk, I noticed a bit of a disturbance behind me, followed by the distinct odor of bleach. I didn't think much of it then. Later it would become more clear to me. We packed up all the last-minute items, checked everybody's life vests for snugness, and hit the river.

The morning went well. We spent much of our time marveling at the steep canyon walls, feeling rather small and insignificant. The rapids were as wild and wonderful as they always were and we had no problems—smooth, clean runs for all. I **did** notice something peculiar in Rubber though. Dave, in his gear boat, had a grimace on his face as he crashed through the towering waves, and it looked as if he was trying most fervently to keep his mouth shut. *Peculiar*, I thought. I had not seen him grimace like that before. Oh well, perhaps he was having a difficult morning. Since he was in a non-self-bailing raft, I figured that he would need some time to bail his boat out below Rubber, so I **eddied out** on the right and waited. He pulled into the **eddy** above us and sat there in his raft, not bailing, just sitting.

"Hey Dave, you need to bail?"

"Nope."

"Are you sure? You look pretty full."

"I'm sure," a tense smile.

"Okay."

Hmmm. Seems odd. What's up with Dave? I thought.

We pulled out of the eddy, Dave pushing his swamped boat out into the current behind us. I didn't think much of it after that. We continued on down the canyon in silence, soaking up as much of the view as we could since this was our last morning on the river.

We reached the confluence with the Main Salmon, turned left, and headed down that wide slide of green water to the take-out at Cache Bar. It was there on the boat ramp that Dave enlightened me about the events of the morning, and it all began to fall into place: the disturbance and smell of bleach, his closed-mouth grimace and unwillingness to bail his boat. I listened to Dave's story with shock and horror.

"I brought the groover down, remember?"

"Yeah."

"And I put it on the **tube** of my boat and then began to make room for it in the **drop deck**. I got it all set up and then I had to kind of, you know, sort of jam it in there because the other **rocket boxes** were kind of in the way. I guess that black plug got stuck on the edge of one of those other boxes but I didn't know that so I just shoved it down in there. I felt it give and then I heard this glug-glug-glug sound and I smelled it, Joe, I smelled it. . . ."

"It's OK, Dave," I said, putting a hand on his shoulder.

"Thanks, Joe. Anyhow, it . . . well it . . . I mean the . . . the. . . ."

"The turds, Dave?"

"Yeah, man, the turds. They just came churning out into the bottom of my boat. Yeaugh! The smell! It was so rank."

"I know, Dave."

"So I quickly tilted the box on its side so it would stop glugging like it was, and then I turned to Beth and I said, 'Beth, uh. I have a situation here,' real calm-like, you know. She came over and saw what was going on and then went and got a bottle of bleach out of the commissary box and emptied it into the bottom of my boat and we threw a couple of buckets of water in there too. This whole time you were just giving your talk and the guests were standing right there, hardly five feet from my boat. I can't believe no one smelled it. Sheesh! It was awful. So then I just tied the rest of the stuff on and we pushed off. I was in kind of a bad mood, you know."

"Of course, Dave. You had good reason."

"And so I decided that I wasn't going to bail my boat till we got to take-out since there were. . . . things floating in there. I figured the more water in the boat the better. As I went through Rubber, the water and bleach and . . . *stuff,* you know, was all splashing around down there and it was getting on my face! I looked down there at one point, Joe, and there were these little bits, these like, little swirlies down there around my ankles. Disgusting! This has just not been my morning."

"I know, Dave. Sorry that happened. We can wash the boat out real well when we get back to town. Thanks for dealing with it so well."

"Sure."

And with that we loaded the trailer and truck, had some lunch, and made the drive back to town.

The next day we had all of the black rubber plugs removed from our Jon-ny Partner groovers and had the holes decisively welded shut.

11

Travesty at Ward's Ferry

Groover Type: *Classic Without Bags*
Rating:

This gem was told to me by a friend, Scott Kazmar. He is a fellow river guide and kayaker and he told me this one recently as we both soaked our sore paddling and hiking muscles in Kern Hot Springs, which is this amazing spring right next to the Kern River in the middle of Sequoia National Park. When he heard that I was writing this book his eyes got big, and he smiled at me through his mustache and said, "I think I've got one for you." Indeed he did. Here it is. Please take note of the rating on this one, though, before reading on. It truly resides in the realm of the six-roller.

Let's go back to the Ward's Ferry Bridge, **take-out** for the Tuolumne River in California, which you may remember from the opening scenes of chapter six, "The Groover That Ate Sonora."

Since the Tuolumne is prematurely plugged by Don Pedro Reservoir, rafters and kayakers running this stream must paddle through a great deal of flat water at the end of their days on the water in order to reach the take-out. In addition to the obstacle of a long flatwater paddle through an ugly reservoir, there is often a logjam that reaches upstream off the lake to the point where the down-canyon current ceases. After pushing their way through hundreds of feet of logs, branches, abandoned Styrofoam coolers, and Mountain Dew cans, the rafts and their occupants sometimes get to paddle for up to three miles in strong afternoon up-canyon winds before reaching Ward's Ferry.

Now, as if this weren't enough toil for one afternoon, when the rafters reach the bridge, they have to carry all of the rafts, coolers, tables, stoves, propane tanks, waterproof bags, and other gear up a long and steep trail before throwing it in a pile on the bridge, which is usually anywhere from 50 to 250 feet above the surface of the reservoir.

Back when I first began working as a raft guide, we used to have our guests hump all of their gear up the trail to the bridge and then come down and help us with the coolers and other gear. In the beginning days of rafting, when things were a little more rugged and prices a little cheaper, we were able to get away with this and bill it as part of the experience, but as the industry began to change and prices went up, we began trying to eliminate such nasty experiences as the Bataan Death March up the hill to Ward's Ferry Bridge.

Our first solution to this problem was to unload the guests at the bridge, from which they were driven to their cars by a guy named Mud in an old, funky bus. Then we'd take on a small ten-horsepower outboard motor, tie all the rafts together, and motor out of the lake, over to Moccasin Point Marina, where we would do our take-out amongst the many houseboats, speedboats, and Budweiser-swilling jet skiers. We often had engine trouble on the lake and several times had to flag down some boat drivers to tow us in;

and even when the engine didn't break, it just took a long time to get to the boat ramp.

But the main problem was that the tow-out across the lake gave the guides too much down time, which they would use to drink all of the leftover beer and have horrendous, mayonnaise-flinging food fights. In fact, one friend of mine, Heidi, used to save particularly slimy tomatoes and other nasty produce items, storing them in a secret spot in one of the coolers so that she could chuck them at her fellow guides on the tow-out.

So, with the tow option, even when it *did* work and the engine did *not* break, the best we could hope for was a bunch of giggling, drunk guides covered in food slime trying to clean and pack up the gear in the headlight glare of our '72 International pickup truck in the dark. Not a pretty sight.

It was obvious what needed to be done—we had to go high-tech. Most of the other rafting outfitters on the Tuolumne had already gone to a winching system for their take-outs, but we had held out, old schoolers until the bitter end. But it was clear now that it was time to join the ranks of the winchers.

A winch rig is really a wonderful thing to use at Ward's Ferry, as it eliminates all of that walking and humping of gear up the hill. It is many times faster and more efficient than towing out on the lake, and it is only possible for guides to drink a few beers before the job is finished. Though excellent, these rigs are kind of expensive, so oftentimes companies will purchase a rig together and share it at the bridge on take-out day.

For our needs, we deemed Big Blue a fine investment: a large, blue, and ugly truck that was used for years by the local telephone company to install telephone poles—and yank them out on occasion. The winch itself is attached to a large boom that the driver swings out over the bridge in order to clear the railing and winch rafts up safely. The truck also has a large stabilizing arm that the driver attaches to the railing on the bridge. This arm steadies the rig so that the weight of the rafts and gear it is winching does not pull it over the railing and down into the lake.

Once the truck is secured, the driver gets into the winching seat, which is kind of like a small crane operator's seat, and he drops the cable over the bridge, lowering it down to the guides waiting in the rafts below. On the end of the cable there are two large loops of firehose big enough to fit entirely around a full-size raft. The guides down in the rafts slide one loop over the bow and one over the stern. The idea is to get the loops evenly placed so that when the driver winches up the load, the raft will not tilt one way or the other but go up flat. As a safety precaution, the guides who are preparing the rafts for winching always get out from beneath the winch when a raft is going up.

The following story details a winching mishap that left its victim alive—though there are some witnesses who report he wished he had died that afternoon instead.

It was the middle of a rather lengthy season and the mercury had been above 100 for about two weeks. The guides working on the bridge were cooking in the sun—but they were used to that. So far, three boats loaded with gear had been winched up and there was only one left. The crew down on the lake beneath the bridge loaded the rafts with gear and placed the firehose loops to ensure safe winching. They moved slowly but efficiently; no reason to move faster than was absolutely necessary. The work would get done.

Some guides from another company that was scheduled to use the winch next had just pulled in and unloaded their guests. The lead guide, Richard, who preferred to be called "Ripper," sat in his raft and, from behind his designer French sunglasses, glared at the guides loading the last raft. It was obvious he was suffering from a glaring case of whitewater-induced egomania—something not uncommon in the death-defying world of river guiding. His hair was long and blond and, of course, he was devilishly handsome.

"Weren't you guys supposed to winch at four?"

"Yeah, sorry, we're a little late."

"Evidently. Just hurry up," said Ripper, and he continued to stare at them.

Now, there is a certain amount of karmic energy on the river that most guides simply refer to as "The River Gods." These gods are, for the most part, very fair in their treatment of those who float down their rivers. However, cocky river guides who think they are getting wiser than the river or who are rude to others are usually dealt with quite swiftly and firmly.

After their short and rather tense conversation with Ripper, the guides loading the raft started to work a little faster. "Almost done," said one guide as he scurried across the loaded raft doing a last minute check of all tie-downs. As he hopped over the load, though, one sandal got caught on the clamping handle of a rocket box and he went sprawling onto the bags and boxes with a thump. Ripper snickered as the other guides helped their friend get up off the load.

"Are you OK?" they asked.

"Yeah." With that, they made their way to the trail and up to the bridge. The guides from the other company then began untying and retying the gear in their rafts, preparing them for winching.

Little did anyone know, but the rocket box whose handle the guide tripped over was, of course, the groover. When he tripped he unhooked the lid on one side, opening the box only slightly.

This groover was a classic without bags, so there was nothing but unbridled turds and paper sludge in that box. Well, actually, there was something else: for some reason, a few of the guests on that trip lacked the necessary muscle control required to poop in the box without peeing in it. Consequently the groover's contents were somewhat liquefied—sort of a caca-peepee slushy.

At first, the raft rose slowly and steadily off the surface of the lake and through the air toward the bridge, spinning slightly on the cable. As soon as it got ten or fifteen feet above the water, Ripper rowed his raft into position below the bridge.

"Hey, Ripper, aren't we supposed to not rig under the winch when they're lifting boats?" inquired one of his crew members sheepishly.

"What are you, scared?"

"Well, no. I just thought it wasn't safe."

"Look, it's no big deal. I've been winching boats here for two years and I've never seen anything happen. Just chill and start getting this boat ready, OK?"

"OK."

And with that, Ripper bent down and continued untying gear and placing items in his raft, securing the load.

Meanwhile, directly above his blonde head, the raft rose heavily through the air, still spinning slightly.

But in their haste to rig the raft and get it winched, the guides had failed to tighten the stern firehose loop sufficiently, and there, seventy feet above the lake—and Ripper—the raft shifted suddenly in the slings and tilted. Though it was still attached to the winch, the boat was noticeably down at the stern.

The breached groover, now tilted, began to purge its contents powerfully, forcing its lid open to a five- or six-inch gap. The reeking shit slushy—perhaps five to seven gallons of human waste and puréed toilet paper—dumped into the bottom of the now listing raft and crept toward the holes in the self-bailing floor. Within seconds, a foul and reeking shower began to fall through the hot air beneath the bridge—liquefied poop and pee cascading silently down to the lake below.

"Christ! Who farted?" asked Ripper.

The other members of his crew just looked up in amazement at the falling veil of shit as it rained down toward their illustrious leader. He didn't have a chance.

Ripper looked up, too, and it was upon him. The bulk of the deluge—a veritable sheet of effluent—landed heavily on his angry upturned face, caking his goatee. His sunglasses were nicely frosted as well.

Every muscle in his body tensed and he screamed so loud that his voice could be heard two miles upstream; the canyon reverberated with his anger.

"Fuuuuuuuuuuuuuuuck!!!!" Shaking his fists in the air, he scrambled for shore.

To everyone's amazement, he elected *not* to jump into the lake and wash the foul mixture from his well-muscled body. Instead, he slowly and steadily walked over the boats to the shore, still repeatedly screaming, "Fuck! Fuck! Fuck! Fuck!" He hiked, fists clenched and jaw set, towards the bridge. The hot sun baked the coating of feces to his skin and hair and by the time he had fumed to the top of the hill and onto the bridge, the coating of turds had dried to his body like a mud pack.

He walked toward the group of horror-stricken guides, his sickening odor preceding him. He stopped and looked straight at them, taking off his shades to reveal hate-filled blue eyes peering out from a foul raccoon's mask. A grimace crept across his face and the dried coating cracked above his lip, dislodging the piece of undigested corn caught in his mustache.

The River Gods had spoken.

12

Last Call: Some Parting Thoughts

The life of the river guide is indeed a charmed one, and I have spent many hours floating through beautiful river canyons wondering why I was getting paid to do it. On the surface, of course, it seems that ours is a job of leisure and vacation and that all we do is row boats down rivers, become bronzed Greek gods and goddesses, and swill cheap beers in camp as we chop vegetables.

While these are parts of the job and the persona, what also comes with the package are a fair amount of grueling work and a number of less-than-glamorous moments. For example, we are often seen elbow deep in the juice of rancid coolers that have been sitting in the heat of the **take-out** vehicle for thirteen too many hours; or pushing on our oars into gale force winds as our guests recline and marvel at the scenery on the banks.

Then there is the sheer *volume* of work to be done. The average river guide rises bleary-eyed at around 6 A.M., boils the water for the coffee, and begins pulling food items from the coolers for a yummy breakfast. He then cooks, cleans, organizes, packs up, loads gear, and runs around camp in a controlled chaotic whirl until everything is loaded and tied onto the rafts. All of this takes somewhere between three and four hours, and by the end of it the sun (or "oppressor" as some guides call it) has been beating down on the back of the toiling guide for some time. His T-shirt has become moist with perspiration and he is usually wishing that he hadn't had that second or third or fourth cup of **cowboy coffee**. He is feeling a tad harried, as this is the end of the morning grind; it's almost time to get back out on that cool, sliding river where he will row his boat, relax, tell stories, take swims, hang out with the guests, and log some more of those stereotypical glorious river-guide moments.

One important morning chore is the break-down of the groover. When I first began guiding, I used to look on this task with disdain, and broke down the box with much wincing and holding of my nose and so forth. But as I have matured I find myself less grossed out by the prospect. I actually look forward to making the rounds through camp reminding the guests and guides that I will be packaging up the goodness soon and that they had better make any last-minute visits. I feel like I am making a connection with everyone on the trip that is a little more meaningful than exchanges like, "good morning," or "nice day."

When I gesture in the direction of the groover trail and say, "Hey, I'm breaking it down now, are you finished?", what I am really saying is, "Do you still need to shit?" As you can see, this is more intimate and personal than your run-of-the-mill morning greeting. I sometimes marvel at who I get to say this to: movie stars, millionaires, foreign diplomats, fellow river guides, and other important and powerful people. It's really quite wonderful.

So after making the rounds and giving the last call, I head up the trail—usually at a slight run, as I am in a hurry to get everything packed and loaded on the boats. At this point I am usually sweaty, dusty, dirty, and feeling a little frazzled. I begin to slow as I prepare for my morning ritual: a poop of my own, groover breakdown, and then it's off for another day at the office.

I approach the box, lift the lid and, of course, I look down in there. I have to. It's part of my childlike curiosity and fascination with poop, I suppose. I always see the same thing but it's kind of interesting to me—just a bunch of turds and T.P., rising in a pile towards the top of the box.

I reflect on how simple the groover is. There are no frills here. It is just a box full of poop, paper, and some bad smells. Shit smells bad. That's a reality I think we sometimes lose touch with in our busy lives. Most of the time, we are simply not connected to ourselves, our families, our communities, or to our bodies and their functions. Our turds are part of us, and creating them is a very human and natural aspect of our being. Perhaps we should take a little time to acknowledge our pieces of poo before flushing them away in crystalline surges of toilet water. In contrast to the traditional toilet, the groover gives us a golden opportunity to come face to face with parts of ourselves that are perhaps a little smelly and not entirely pleasant. I believe Carl Jung would refer to these aspects as the Shadow, the darker side of the self. I really don't feel like getting into what Sigmund Freud would say about it.

After pondering the pile, I pull down my shorts and sit on the seat. I relax and soak up the view that surrounds me: a grove of large, red-barked ponderosa pines shading me and swaying in the morning breeze; the river beyond the trees flowing powerfully by, a clear and swift ribbon of liquid glass; and rising up all around me, the canyon itself, a granite cathedral yawning toward the morning sky. All of my concerns fade away and I begin to feel my place in the greater scheme. I hear the descending call of the canyon wren and see a squirrel scurry along through the underbrush. Sitting and pondering my connection to these other beasts, I marvel at the beauty around me. My mind drifts to one of Henry David Thoreau's wisest pieces of advice, "simplify, simplify, simplify." And what could be more basic and real than sitting in the woods, admiring the splendor of a river canyon, and taking a dump?

This simplicity is, to me, the greatest lure of my chosen life. In this day and age, when we jet around the globe in flying machines and down the highway in little metal boxes on wheels, when we eat empty food cooked by microwaves, perhaps what many of us need and crave most is a little bit of unfettered simplicity. What could be more appealing than a true break from the trappings of our artificial, "virtual" world? In the wilderness, everything is *real*: when it rains you get wet; when the temperature drops, you get cold. On the river, we sit around a fire and hear stories told by a storyteller at night, engage in conversations, gaze at the stars burning in cold space hundreds of light-years away— and we crap in a box and take it down the river with us.

I sit on the groover a moment after finishing, wipe, and rise. I hoist my shorts and admire my creation. I feel considerably better now—relieved. I have appreciated a wonderful view, thought some good thoughts, and taken a fine dump. I see the contributions of others and I see the groover at that moment as more than just a can of crap. I see it as a mosaic of the many and varied people on the trip. We are all individuals making singular contributions, but together we are something much larger.

The groover is also a great equalizer. The simple fact is that everyone poops. Regardless of who we are, how much money we make, who we're sleeping with, what we look like, or how straight our teeth are, once a day, sometimes more, sometimes less, we all sit or squat and take a crap. The president does it. The queen does it. Mother Theresa does it. The Pope does it. Bears do it. We all do it.

I squeeze the air from the liner bags, directing the flow of foul air away from my nose and mouth, and tie knots in the plastic bags. Nice, tight knots. I put the toilet paper in a Ziploc bag, refold the *National Enquirer* (standard groover reading) before placing it on top of the collection of pods in the can, slide the seat down the side, and seal the **rocket box** with its metal clamping lid. Breakdown is a done deal.

The walk down the trail is a pleasant one, and I welcome gratefully the smell of the incense cedar. The bustle has continued in camp in my absence and the boats are all ready to go, save for the groover rig. I make my way through camp and down to the beach, where many of the guests are relaxing in the sun, chatting, and looking at the river map, in preparation for another day of floating through the canyons. I see that there is a clear path away from all of them, but I also see that I could walk straight through the group with my burden. I decide on the more adventurous line and make my way for the heart of the group.

They see me coming and conversation stops. I feel their eyes upon me but I just pretend I don't notice and walk straight up to and through the group, saying nothing. Someone says, "Hey there. Careful with that, Joe!" and everybody laughs and there are some more comments: "Don't drop that one!"; "Eeeew!"; and a smattering of poop jokes amongst nervous laughter. I fake a trip and say "Whoah!" before regaining my balance and making my way to the **gear raft** where I tie that baby down—tie it down well so as not to provide any more tales for the second edition of this book.

Then I walk over to my oar boat, get in, sit down on my cooler, place my cap on my head, put on a little sunscreen, grab the oars in my hands, look up- and downriver, and check with the other guides to see if they are ready to pull out of the **eddy**. I take a deep breath and as I exhale, a smile stretches across my face and I say what I love to say when I am in these places, doing these things: "Just another day at the office." And with that, I pull out into the current and around the bend with my load of food, people, and, of course, poo.

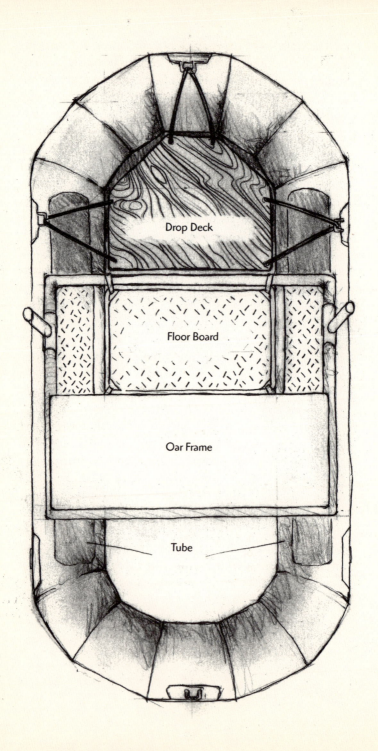

Drop Deck

Floor Board

Oar Frame

Tube

Glossary

Alpenglow The orangeish-pink light that bathes granite peaks and mountains in early morning and late evening.

Ammo can A small metal box that is used by the military to keep bullets dry. These are wonderful watertight containers and are used for storing and organizing many things on river trips.

Bail bucket A large five-gallon plastic bucket that delis and restaurants use to hold their pickles and olives. River people use them to bail water out of *non-self-bailing* rafts as well as for many other things. Some have even used them as groovers, which is kind of nasty.

Blue goo An odor retardant and decomposer that river people sometimes add to their groovers to keep the smell down and to reduce gas buildup in the groover, thus reducing the chance of an unforeseen explosion.

Burping the bags A rather unsavory responsibility of the guide charged with breaking down the classic groover with bags. Before tying the knots in the bags, the guide must squeeze, or "burp," all of the air out of the poo *pod.*

Commissary box Usually a rather large and ungainly metal box that contains all of the pots, pans, utensils, spices, and other cooking items necessary for crafting gourmet meals out in the middle of nowhere.

Cowboy coffee Rather strong coffee; it is made by boiling water and throwing in ground coffee, which is then sunk to the bottom using one or more of the following techniques: swinging the pot back and forth by its wire handle; banging the side of the pot with a pair of pliers; dropping egg shells onto or sprinkling cold water into the brown sludgy mixture. Regardless of the method, the end product is a sometimes chewy but always hearty cup of coffee. Some less rugged river guides have suggested—and even had the gall to *use* —jelly strainers to sift out coffee grounds when pouring, but this is universally recognized as a habit of cream puffs and pansies. I think you can see where the author stands on this issue.

Drop deck A piece of ¾-inch plywood that is slung in the middle compartment of a *gear raft*, about 3 inches above the floor. Packages, boxes, and bags of river gear are then tied down to it.

Dutch oven A large cast-iron pot with a lid that is used to cook biscuits, baklava, lasagna, brownies, and corn bread, among other things. Coals are placed on the ground and the "d.o." is set on top of these. More coals are then put on the lid, heating the oven evenly. Dutch ovens are often used in river cooking.

Eddy A flat section of river that actually flows upstream. They form behind rocks and islands in the middle of the current or along the banks.

Eddy out The term for when a raft guide steers his or her boat into an eddy. The guide usually does this to take a break, to look around, or maybe to stop for camp or for lunch.

Gear raft A raft that is rigged with large wooden oars and a frame that enables one guide to row the boat all by herself with no assistance from paddlers.

Goodness Euphemism for shit.

Groover A toilet used on wilderness river trips.

Hoopie Commonly referred to as tubular webbing, but we rafter types call it "hoopie." With it, we tie everything together and down on our boats, on our cars, and generally in our lives.

Non-self-bailing raft The kind of raft featured in "Swirlies at His Ankles." It has a flat bottom, and the water must be bailed out of it with *bail buckets*.

Oar frame A collection of various pipes, nuts, bolts, and pieces of wood that, when assembled and tied to a raft, provides many slots and nooks and crannies into which camping and rafting gear can be stuffed. The oar frame provides stability and structure to a raft and also has towers to which large wooden oars are attached.

Paddle raft A raft that has no gear or rowing frame—just a rubber raft. Each person in the boat is given a paddle and they all work together to get the boat down the river.

Pod A package of human poop, sealed in two large garbage bags. These are produced by the classic groover with bags and are usually the size of a cantaloupe.

Polypro This is short for polypropylene long underwear, which river guides wear quite often as it keeps them warm even when they're wet. It is amazing material. Unfortunately it has an "odor memory" and will retain the essense of its wearer even after repeated washings. A friend of mine, Animal, once keel-hauled his polypro for six days on the Middle Fork of the Salmon but to no avail. I believe he had to throw it out. Well, he should have.

Pooper Yet another euphemism for the *groover*.

Put-in The starting point of a river trip.

Rocket Boxes These are larger versions of *ammo cans*.

Self-bailing raft This is a raft equipped with an inflatable floor and grommet holes around the sides that enable water to exit when taken aboard, thus bailing itself. The water comes into the raft and is immediately purged through the holes.

Shuttle The drive, flight, or bike ride from the *take-out* back to the *put-in* where vehicles are stored.

Take-out The ending point of a river trip, where all the rafts and gear are packed up and piled into old trucks that are prone to breaking down.

Tamarisk A non-native plant that was introduced into the desert Southwest in the last century. It has done very well in Grand Canyon, especially since 1968 when the Glen Canyon Dam was finished and Glen Canyon inundated. The natural floods that would normally rip out the "tammies," as they are sometimes called, do not happen any longer, so the plants have thrived and spread through the Canyon, crowding out the native riparian shrubs.

Trucker's hitch This is a knot that river guides use frequently. When tied with a certain amount of strength, it can make a very tight line.

Tube (Go to the picture of the raft on page 76 for this one.)

Wrapping a raft When a raft hits a rock sideways and the current shoves its downstream side up the rock, its upstream side down the rock, under water, and its bow and stern around the sides—shrink-wrapping it to the rock like the cellophane on a sandwich in a convenience store. To unwrap these rafts, guides use common sense, groovy shiny climbing gear, thick ropes, humility, and a generous amount of cursing. There is a river guide mantra that says there are only three types of guides: those who have wrapped, those who will, and those who will again. Wrapping and flipping are the two classic river wipe-outs.

A Real Fun Collection of Shit Words and Phrases

Words

B.M.
caca
coil
corn-backed rattler
corn-eyed brown trout
crap
doo-doo
dookie
feces
floater
goodness
growler
load
loaf
log
number two
poo
poop
poo-poo
scat
shit
sinker
soft-serve
steamer
stool
turd

Phrases

I gotta . . .
coil one
crank a rad
download the database
drop a load
drop a log
drop the kids off at the pool
grind a steamer
grow a tail
lay some cable
lay some pipe
make stinky
pinch a loaf
push one through the hoops
release the hostage
steam one
take a dump
unleash the kraken

More books from Ten Speed Press

How to Shit in the Woods
Second Edition
by Kathleen Meyer
With half a million copies in print, HOW TO SHIT IN THE
WOODS is the beloved classic of no-nonsense environmental
awareness.
5 x 8½ inches, 128 pages, paperback

Cuthbertson's All-In-One Bike Repair Manual
by Tom Cuthbertson
The fully revised and updated edition of ANYBODY'S BIKE
BOOK (750,000 in print) is geared to the owners of road bikes,
mountain bikes, and cruisers.
6 x 9 inches, 240 pages, paperback

The 2 Oz. Backpacker
A Problem Solving Manual for Use in the Wilds
by Robert S. Woods
"The closest thing to a hiker's bible I've ever come across. . . ."
 —Northwest Books
4 x 6½ inches, 128 pages, paperback

Mushrooms Demystified
by David Arora
Simply the best and most complete field guide and reference book,
with over 950 photographs; 55,000 copies in print.
6 x 9 inches, 1020 pages, paperback or cloth

Psylocybin Mushrooms of the World
An Identification Guide
by Paul Stamets. Foreword by Andrew Weil
The only identification guide exclusively devoted to psilocybin-con-
taining mushrooms worldwide, with detailed descriptions and color
photos of over 100 species.
6 x 9 inches, 256 pages, paperback

For more information, or to order, call the publisher at the number
below. We accept VISA, Mastercard, and American Express. You
may also wish to write for our free catalog of over 500 books,
posters, and audiotapes.

Ten Speed Press
P.O. Box 7123, Berkeley, CA 94707
800-841-BOOK